Black and White Photographs to Instagram

Then to Now Tech

By Jennifer Colby

21st Century Junior Library

Published in the United States of America by
Cherry Lake Publishing
Ann Arbor, Michigan
www.cherrylakepublishing.com

Content Adviser: Adam Fulton Johnson, PhD History of Science and Technology, University of Michigan
Reading Adviser: Marla Conn, MS, Ed., Literacy specialist, Read-Ability, Inc.

Photo Credits: ©James Steidl/Shutterstock.com, Cover, 1 [left]; ©Ink Drop/Shutterstock.com, Cover, 2 [right]; ©Everett Historical/Shutterstock.com, 4; ©LiliGraphie/Shutterstock.com, 6; ©Everett Historical/Shutterstock.com, 8; ©Mark Jennings-bates/Shutterstock.com, 10; ©Lenscap Photography/Shutterstock.com, 12; ©Djordje Novakov/Shutterstock.com, 14; ©Enrique Alcala/Shutterstock.com, 16; ©Dean Drobot/ Shutterstock.com, 18; ©Branislav Nenin/Shutterstock.com, 20

Library of Congress Cataloging-in-Publication Data
Names: Colby, Jennifer, 1971- author.
Title: Black and white photographs to Instagram / Jennifer Colby.
Description: Ann Arbor : Cherry Lake Publishing, [2019] | Series: Then to now tech | Includes bibliographical references and index. | Audience: K to grade 3.
Identifiers: LCCN 2019004218 | ISBN 9781534147249 (hardcover) | ISBN 9781534148673 (pdf) | ISBN 9781534150102 (pbk.) | ISBN 9781534151536 (hosted ebook)
Subjects: LCSH: Photography–History–Juvenile literature.
Classification: LCC TR149 .C64 2019 | DDC 770–dc23
LC record available at https://lccn.loc.gov/2019004218

Cherry Lake Publishing would like to acknowledge the work of the Partnership for 21st Century Skills. Please visit *www.p21.org* for more information.

Printed in the United States of America
Corporate Graphics

CONTENTS

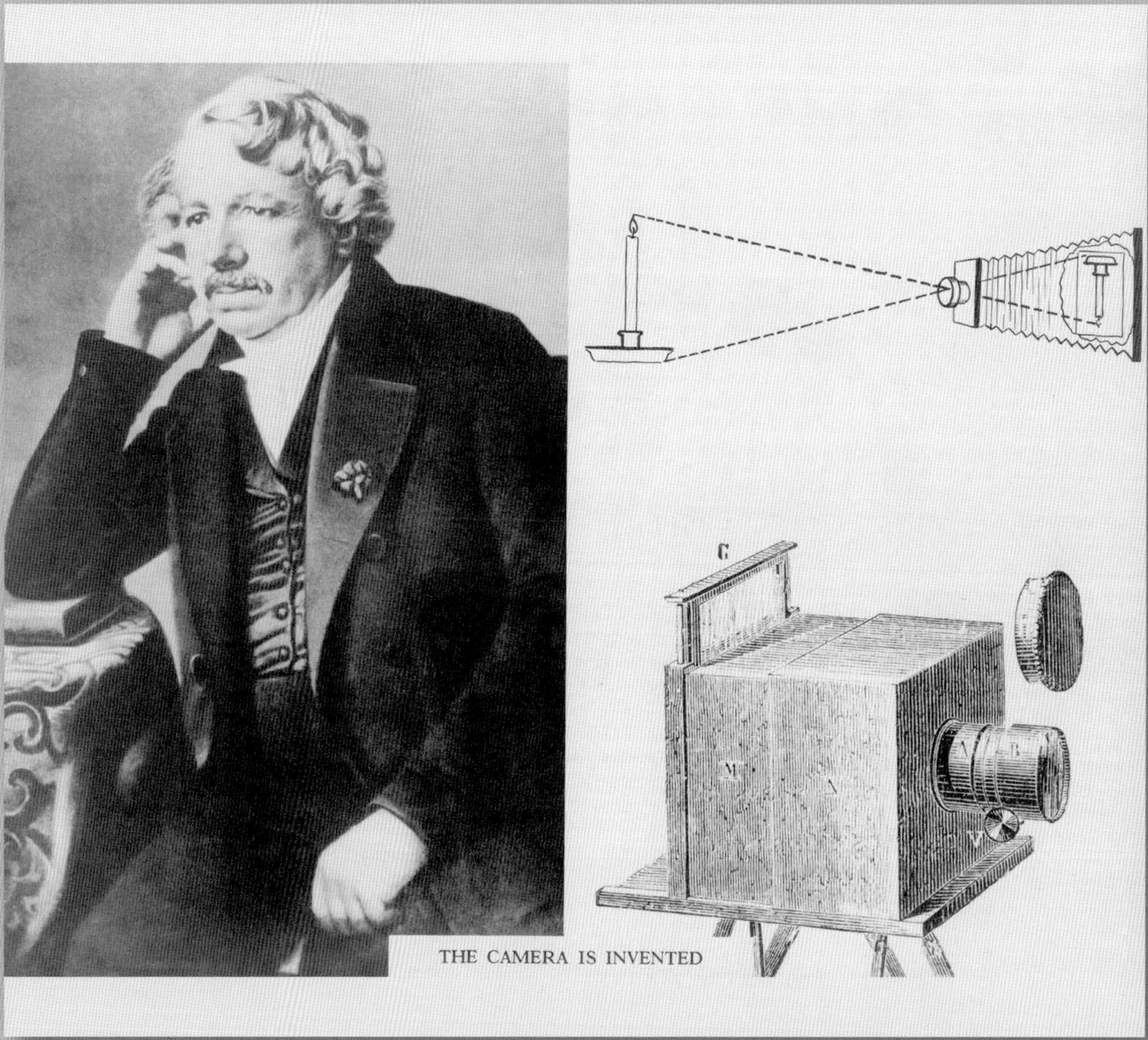

Louis Daguerre's invention started with an illustration.

Captured Images

During the 18th century, **inventors** tried to record images as seen by the human eye. These attempts were not very successful. Then in 1839, Frenchman Louis Daguerre created a **process** for making a clear and **permanent** black and white image from a camera that only took minutes. He named it the **daguerreotype** after himself.

Why is no one smiling? Getting a photograph taken
was a serious event.

Say CHEESE!

Most early **photographs** show very serious people. This could be for many reasons. One popular belief has to do with **oral hygiene**. People of the 19th century might not have smiled because their mouths were full of rotten teeth! They didn't brush or floss their teeth regularly like we do today. However, other people think there are better reasons why no one smiled.

Even presidents needed to get their portraits taken!

Another reason could be because it took time to **capture** a photographic image. At first, people needed to sit still for 20 minutes or else the photo would be blurry. Later, this **exposure** time was reduced to as little as 20 seconds. But most likely, people looked serious because getting your photo taken was a very formal **occasion**. It wasn't a time for having fun.

Look!

Ask an older relative to show you photos of your **ancestors**. Are they smiling in their photographs?

Kodak's Brownie was a very popular early box camera.

Photography for Everyone

Numerous improvements in photography happened over time. Equipment became cheaper and easier to use. Color **film** was invented. And film could be sent out for **developing**.

In 1888, the Kodak Company sold the first popular box camera. It was very easy to use. The company's slogan was, "You press the button, we do the rest." Similar easy-to-use cameras were soon produced and sold all over the world.

Color film became popular in the mid-20th century.

At first, the process for developing color photography took a lot of effort! A photographer had to take the same image multiple times on separate color plates. In 1935, Kodak introduced film that could take a full-color photo with one push of a button. Soon many other companies sold color film.

For many years, photographers had to develop their black and white photos themselves. This was a multi-step process that required dangerous chemicals in a darkroom.

Polaroid introduced instant cameras in 1948.

In the 1960s, photo developing shops began to open up all around the world. It became easy to get your color film developed into photographs. Some cameras even developed the photo inside the camera right after you took the picture!

Ask Questions!

Have you ever seen a photography darkroom? Ask your older friends and family if they have ever seen or used a darkroom before.

A digital camera has a screen that shows the image that is being captured.

Going Digital

Digital cameras became widely available in the 1990s. Soon they became more popular than film cameras. Digital cameras require no film and can store thousands of images.

Think!

How are digital images recorded? Ask an adult to help you search the internet to find out.

We take photos and post them on social media every day. Selfies are popular. Have you taken one?

Today, smartphones have almost replaced digital cameras. With a smartphone camera, you can take and share photos anywhere. Its ability to connect to different social media **platforms**, like Instagram, allow you to immediately share photos with family and friends.

Instagram began in 2010 and has become one of the world's most popular photo-sharing **apps**. On the day the Instagram app was released for Android phones, it was downloaded over 1 million times!

The future of photography may be in its past.

As photography advances, some people prefer the artistic effort required by older cameras. Others look forward to smaller cameras—so small they can be made into contact lenses! No matter what cameras are used in the future, capturing images will always be popular.

Make a Guess!

New digital cameras may be controlled by eye movements! How do you think this would work? Ask an adult to help you search the internet to see if your guess is right.

GLOSSARY

ancestors (AN-ses-turz) people who were in someone's family in past times

apps (APS) computer programs that perform special functions

capture (KAP-chur) to record something in a picture

daguerreotype (duh-GAIR-uh-tipe) an old type of photograph that was made on a piece of silver or a piece of copper covered in silver

developing (dih-VEL-uhp-ing) treating film with chemicals to bring out the photos that were taken using it

exposure (ik-SPOH-zhur) the amount of time during which light is allowed to enter a camera in order to produce a photograph

film (FILM) a special material that is used for taking photographs

inventors (in-VEN-turz) people who create or produce something useful for the first time

occasion (uh-KAY-zhuhn) a particular time when something happens

oral hygiene (OR-uhl HYE-jeen) the practice of keeping teeth and gums in a healthy condition

permanent (PUR-muh-nuhnt) lasting or continuing for a very long time or forever

photographs (FOH-tuh-grafs) pictures made by a camera

platforms (PLAT-formz) computer programs that allow for the sharing of information

process (PRAH-ses) a series of actions that produce something

FIND OUT MORE

BOOKS

Anderson, Jennifer Joline. *Should Kids Use Social Media?* Chicago: Norwood House Press, 2018.

Hockney, David. *A History of Pictures for Children: From Cave Paintings to Computer Drawings*. New York: Harry N. Abrams, 2018.

WEBSITES

Canva—Black and White Photography: Seeing Beyond Color
https://www.canva.com/learn/seeing-beyond-color-learn-masters-black-white-photography-7-practical-tips
Learn tips and techniques from the masters of black and white photography.

KidsHealth—Teaching Kids to Be Smart About Social Media
https://kidshealth.org/en/parents/social-media-smarts.html
Learn the good and the bad of social media and how to stay safe.

INDEX

ABOUT THE AUTHOR

Jennifer Colby is a school librarian in Ann Arbor, Michigan. She loves reading, traveling, and going to museums to learn about new things.